AIRPLANES

By Patricia Lantier-Sampon
Illustrated by Timothy Spransy

Gareth Stevens Publishing
MILWAUKEE

For a free color catalog describing Gareth Stevens' list of high-quality books, call 1-800-341-3569 (USA) or 1-800-461-9120 (Canada).

Library of Congress Cataloging-in-Publication Data

Lantier-Sampon, Patricia.
     Airplanes / by Patricia Lantier-Sampon; illustrated by
Timothy Spransy.
        p. cm. — (Wings)
     Includes index.
     ISBN 0-8368-0539-9
     1. Airplanes—Juvenile literature. [1. Airplanes.] I. Spransy,
Timothy, ill. II. Title. III. Series.
TL547.L423   1994
629.133'34—dc20   91-50344

Edited, designed, and produced by
Gareth Stevens Publishing
1555 North RiverCenter Drive, Suite 201
Milwaukee, Wisconsin 53212, USA

Designer: Kristi Ludwig

Printed in the United States of America

1 2 3 4 5 6 7 8 9 99 98 97 96 95 94

Contents

Airplanes are wonderful flying machines. They soar way up high in the sky.

Passenger Planes

Passenger planes carry people (and pets!) — some pulled by propellers, some driven by jets.

Fighter Planes

Fighter planes savagely zip, zap, and zoom. They slash through the sky with a big sonic BOOM!

Cargo Planes

Cargo planes carry huge, heavy loads — supplies and equipment, machines that build roads.

Yesterday's Planes

Yesterday's planes looked dapper and dandy. Their trusty propellers were really quite handy!

Sport Planes

Sport planes can twirl and dip to the ground.

Now hold your breath, folks, while
we flip upside down!

Crop Dusters

Crop dusters sputter and roar and spray. Farmers can use them to keep bugs away.

Spy Planes

Spy planes silently slip through
the sky. They snap secret
pictures while flying up high.

Seaplanes

Seaplanes are agile, part plane and part boat. What fun it must be to fly first, and then float!

The Concorde

The Concorde has stately, elegant poise. It breaks the sound barrier with a deafening noise.

Spaceplanes

Spaceplanes may soon shuttle people through space. They'll speed through the ozone with barely a trace.

Airplanes are wonderfully grand
and exciting. Isn't it fun to
have wings?

Glossary

agile: able to move quickly and easily.

atmosphere: the mixture of gases surrounding our planet.

ozone: a protective layer of gas in the Earth's atmosphere.

sonic boom: a loud noise, like an explosion, that happens when aircraft travel faster than the speed of sound.

sound barrier: the speed of sound. When aircraft break the sound barrier, it means they are traveling faster than the speed of sound.

Index